Horses

Lipizzan Horses

by Kim O'Brien

Consulting Editor: Gail Saunders-Smith, PhD

Mankato, Minnesota

Pebble Books are published by Capstone Press,
151 Good Counsel Drive, P.O. Box 669, Mankato, Minnesota 56002.
www.capstonepress.com

Books published by Capstone Press are manufactured with paper
containing at least 10 percent post-consumer waste.

Library of Congress Cataloging-in-Publication Data
O'Brien, Kim, 1960–
    Lipizzan horses / by Kim O'Brien.
    p. cm. — (Pebble books. Horses.)
    Includes bibliographical references and index.
    Summary: "A brief introduction to the characteristics, life cycle, and uses of the
Lipizzan horse breed" — Provided by publisher.
    ISBN-13: 978-1-4296-3305-5 (library binding)
    1. Lipizzaner horse — Juvenile literature. I. Title. II. Series.
SF293.L5O27 2010
636.1'38—dc22   2008048889

Note to Parents and Teachers

The Horses set supports national science standards related to life
science. This book describes and illustrates the Lipizzan horse.
The images support early readers in understanding the text.
The repetition of words and phrases helps early readers learn
new words. This book also introduces early readers to
subject-specific vocabulary words, which are defined in the
Glossary section. Early readers may need assistance to read some
words and to use the Table of Contents, Glossary, Read More,
Internet Sites, and Index sections of the book.

Table of Contents

Dancing Horse. 5

From Foal to Adult 9

Performing. 13

Gentle Horses 19

Glossary 22

Read More 23

Internet Sites. 23

Index 24

4

Dancing Horse

Lipizzans are horses
that can learn to dance.
This smart breed prances
and leaps into the air.

6

Lipizzans are gray in color
but look white.
They have strong legs
and thick, curved necks.

From Foal to Adult

Lipizzan foals are born
with dark brown
or black coats.
Their coats get lighter
as they age.

Adult Lipizzans
are shorter
than most breeds.
They stand 14 to 15
hands tall.

Horses are measured in hands.
Each hand is 4 inches (10 centimeters).
A horse is measured from the ground
to its withers.

Performing

Lipizzans perform in shows.
They stand on their hind legs
and do other moves.

Lipizzans perform to music.
They leap and step high
to the beat.

16

Teams of Lipizzans
dance together.
They move in patterns
and march together.

Gentle Horses

Lipizzans make
good harness horses.
These calm horses
pull carriages in
busy cities and parks.

Lipizzans have
a gentle nature.
Lipizzans and their riders
become good friends.

Glossary

breed — a group of animals that come from common relatives

carriage — a large cart with wheels that is often pulled by horses

foal — a young horse

harness — a set of leather straps that connect a horse to a cart or wagon

hind — the back or rear of something

march — to walk together in an orderly way

nature — an animal's personality

prance — to walk or move in a lively or proud way

Read More

Kama Einhorn. *My First Book about Horses and Ponies.*
New York: Random House, 2008.

Pitts, Zachary. *The Pebble First Guide to Horses.*
First Guides. Mankato, Minn.: Capstone Press, 2009.

Internet Sites

FactHound offers a safe, fun way to find Internet sites
related to this book. All of the sites on FactHound have been
researched by our staff.

Here's all you do:

Visit *www.facthound.com*

FactHound will fetch the best sites for you!

Index

breed, 5, 11
carriages, 19
coats, 9
color, 7, 9
dancing, 5, 15, 17
foals, 9
hands, 11
harness, 19

legs, 7, 13
marching, 17
music, 15
necks, 7
performing, 13, 15
prancing, 5
teams, 17
withers, 11

Word Count: 129
Grade: 1
Early-Intervention Level: 19

Editorial Credits
Sarah L. Schuette, editor; Bobbi J. Wyss, designer; Jo Miller, media researcher

Photo Credits
Alamy/blickwinkel, 8; Ian Middleton, 18; Juniors Bildarchiv, cover, 4, 10
fotolia/Martin, 1, 6
Getty Images Inc/AFP/Timothy A. Clary, 20; Business Wire/Handout, 12
Landov LLC/Reuters/Eddie Keogh, 16
Newscom, 14

The author dedicates this book in memory of her grandmother, Katherine
Boulware Sutton.